Christmas

Celebrating Life, Giving, and Kindness

Arlene Erlbach

Enslow Publishers, Inc.
40 Industrial Road   PO Box 38
Box 398   Aldershot
Berkeley Heights, NJ 07922 Hants GU12 6BP
USA   UK
          http://www.enslow.com

Dedicated to Bob Johnson and Cindy Philbin, who know how to do a great December production. Special thanks to Reverend Greg Bostrum and Reverend Cathy Bostrum. Congratulations to Ms. Paula Bachman and to Matt on the Bach oratorio.

Library of Congress Cataloging-in-Publication Data

Erlbach, Arlene.
Christmas—celebrating life, giving, and kindness / Arlene Erlbach.
    p. cm. – (Finding out about holidays)
ISBN 0-7660-1576-9
1. Christmas—Juvenile literature. 2. Christmas—United States—Juvenile literature.
[1. Christmas.] I. Title. II. Series.
GT4985.5 .E75 2001
394.2663'0973—dc21
    00-010375

Printed in the United States of America

10 9 8 7 6 5 4 3 2 1

To Our Readers:
All Internet Addresses in this book were active and appropriate when we went to press. Any comments or suggestions can be sent by e-mail to Comments@enslow.com or to the address on the back cover.

Photo Credits: Archive Photos, pp. 24, 25 (top right), 31, 32, 47; Archive Photos/Lambert, p. 20; CNP/Archive Photos, p. 34; Corel Corporation, pp. 1, 2, 3, 4, 6, 7 (top), 8, 9, 10, 16, 17, 18, 21, 23, 28 (top), 30, 31 (top), 36, 37, 38, 39, 40, 41, 46, 48; Hemera Technologies Inc., 1997–2000, pp. 5, 7 (bottom), 11, 15, 19, 22, 27, 28 (bottom), 33, 35, 42, 43, 44, 45; Hulton Getty Collection/Archive Photos, pp. 12 (both), 13 (both), 14; National Archives, p. 29; Popperfoto/Archive Photos, pp. 25 (bottom left), 26.

Cover Photo: Corel Corporation (background and all inset photos).

CONTENTS

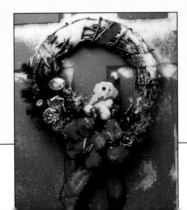

Every year, toward the end of December, millions of people all over the world look forward to Christmas.

CHAPTER 1

A Very Popular Holiday

There is a town in Indiana that is known as Santa Claus. At the town's entrance there is a giant statue of Santa Claus. It is twenty-five feet tall and weighs about forty tons. Each year the post office in Santa Claus, Indiana, gets about 5 million pieces of holiday mail.

Every December millions of people all over the world wait for the twenty-fifth day of the month. They are looking forward to Christmas, one of the most celebrated holidays of the year.

As the day of Christmas gets closer, many children and their families prepare for the holiday. They may write letters to Santa Claus, hoping he will bring them gifts. Children and adults send cards to family and friends. More than 4 billion Christmas cards go through the United States Post Office each year.

At school, children make projects during

Some children write letters to Santa Claus to let him know what kinds of presents to bring for Christmas.

December, featuring Christmas crafts and ideas. They may participate in holiday assemblies, too. Some children collect clothes or food to give to people who need them. Many schools close for winter vacation during the days between Christmas and New Year's Day. The day before school ends, children often attend classroom parties. These celebrations may include a gift exchange or a visit from Santa Claus.

Christmas customs differ from place to place. They vary from family to family, too. Some people put up a Christmas tree right after Thanksgiving. Other families wait until Christmas is closer—or until Christmas Eve, the night before Christmas. Many families exchange gifts and attend church services on Christmas Eve.

During the weeks before Christmas, many homes are decorated. Some families treat the holiday in a more religious manner. They might display nativity scenes, depicting the birth of Jesus who was born more than two thousand years ago.

No matter how people celebrate Christmas,

In the weeks before Christmas arrives, many families like to decorate a Christmas tree to be displayed inside their home.

No matter how people celebrate Christmas, they are honoring the birth of Jesus, the founder of the Christian religion.

they share a tradition with many people all over the world. They are honoring the birth of Jesus Christ, the founder of the Christian religion. It is the world's largest religion with more than a billion members. The word *Christmas* means "Mass of Christ." A Mass is a prayer service.

Some people go to church on Christmas Day to celebrate the birth of Jesus.

Christmas is celebrated all over the world on December 25. But, no one really knows for sure the exact month and date that Jesus was born.

Christmas Becomes a Holiday

Many countries count time starting from the birth of Christ. The United States is one of the countries that uses this system. The years after Christ's birth are named with the letters A.D. before the year. A.D. stands for Anno Domini. It means "in the year of our Lord." The letters B.C. after a year stand for "before Christ."

Christians around the world celebrate Christ's birth on December 25. However, nobody knows for sure the month and date of Jesus's birth. His birth date was based on a different calendar than the one we use today. He may have been born during another month of the year.

What we do know about Christ's birth comes from a part of the Bible called the New Testament. According to the Bible, a couple named Mary and Joseph lived in the village of Nazareth. The town is now part of a country called Israel. At that time, Nazareth was part of

A part of the Bible known as the New Testament tells us all about Christ's birth.

The baby Jesus sits on Joseph's lap.

an area known as Judea, and Judea was ruled by Romans.

An angel told Mary she would have a baby. The baby would be named Jesus, and he would be God's son. Near the time of the baby's birth, Mary and Joseph needed to travel to Bethlehem, a town about one hundred miles from their home. Mary and Joseph planned to sleep at an inn when they reached Bethlehem. But the inn had no room for them. Instead, the innkeeper allowed them to stay in the stable.

Mary gave birth to her baby in the stable and named him Jesus. She used a manger, a feed box for animals, for his bed. A magical star appeared in the sky. Three wise men followed the star to the stable. They brought Jesus gifts. Angels told shepherds about the birth of Jesus. The shepherds came to the stable to see Jesus. Then, they spread the news about the birth of God's son.

When Jesus grew up, he became a preacher. He told people to love one another. He taught people that they should be kind to one another. He healed the blind and the sick. People who believed that Jesus was the son of God became his followers. His closest followers were called apostles. Jesus had twelve apostles. They taught his lessons to many people.

Many people believed in Jesus and his teachings, but he had enemies, too. Not everyone believed that he was God's son. Pontius Pilate, the Roman governor of Judea, feared that Jesus might lead a revolt against the Romans. He wanted Jesus dead. The governor sentenced Jesus to be crucified. He was nailed to two wooden poles that formed a cross, and

When baby Jesus was born, a magical star appeared in the sky. Three wise men followed the star to the baby.

As a boy, Jesus learned how to be a carpenter in Joseph's carpentry shop in Nazareth.

he remained there until he died. His body was then placed in a tomb. The Bible tells that Jesus came back to life for several weeks. Then, he rose to heaven to be with God, his father.

After Jesus's death, many people followed Christianity, the religion that he had founded.

But many early Christians followed pagan ways, too. This means they worshiped more than one god. They believed that these gods controlled natural events such as daylight, darkness, and the seasons. These people observed both their older pagan festivals and the newer Christian celebrations.

Christian priests wanted Christians to stop celebrating pagan holidays. They wanted the people to celebrate only Christian holidays. Christmas seems to have replaced pagan festivals that ancient people held in late December. These holidays honored the return of the sun.

For people who live in the Northern Hemisphere, winter begins on December 21 or 22. The first day of winter is the shortest day of the year. This is because the planet Earth is

Christmas seems to have replaced pagan festivals held in December.

Some people who lived long ago thought the sun might not always return. They held festivals to honor the gods they believed controlled the sun.

at a point where it is tilted farthest away from the sun, and less sunlight reaches Earth. As winter approaches, the hours of daylight gradually become less. A few days after winter begins, Earth tilts closer to the sun. Then, Earth begins to receive more sunlight. So, daytime becomes longer.

Some people who lived long ago thought the sun might not always return. During this time, they held festivals honoring the gods that they believed controlled the sun. People hoped by doing this, the sun would be sure to return.

Romans held a festival called Saturnalia. It honored Saturn, the god of farming. It ended on December 25, with a holiday called the Birthday of the Unconquered Sun. During

Saturnalia, people held feasts and gave gifts. Northern European people celebrated a similar holiday called Yule. Persians honored Mithra, the goddess of light, at this time of year.

Many early Christians celebrated holidays honoring the return of the sun and the birthday of Christ. They did not always observe Christmas in early winter, though. Some people celebrated Christmas in the spring.

About three hundred years after Christ's birth, Christian leaders in Rome said the date for Christ's birthday should be December 25. December 25 was already a holiday in the Roman Empire. It was the Birthday of the Unconquered Sun. Church leaders probably hoped that Christians would

About three hundred years after the birth of Christ, Christian leaders in Rome set December 25 as his official birth date.

stop celebrating this holiday and celebrate Christmas instead.

Gradually, people began celebrating Christmas, instead of honoring the return of the sun. But they celebrated Christmas

This church choir sings festive songs for Christmas.

differently than we do now. Christian priests wanted it to be a day for prayers, not a day to have fun.

Five hundred years after Christ's birth, the pope, the leader of the Catholic Church, held three prayer services in Rome, Italy, on December 25. He called them Masses. The first one was held at midnight. The second one was at sunrise. The third came later in the day. But, unlike Christmas today, nobody went home to a house full of decorations and gifts.

Hundreds of years ago, people celebrated Christmas differently than we do today.

19

The reflection in this Christmas tree ornament shows the scene as it might have appeared at the birth of Christ in the stable.

CHAPTER 3

Santa Claus Brings Gifts

Even after the Catholic Church set a date and a serious tone for Christmas, some people continued to give gifts. The idea of giving gifts at Christmas was part of the earlier holidays honoring the return of the sun. Christian priests did not like this idea. Gift giving was a symbol of the holiday they wanted Christians to give up. But it did not stop. Eventually, it was connected to a man named Saint Nicholas. He was later replaced by the figure known as Santa Claus.

Saint Nicholas was a Christian bishop. He lived around A.D. 300. He was known as a friend

to sailors, the poor, and children. After his death in A.D. 343, he was remembered for the good deeds he had done during his life. He became a saint, a holy person or a religious hero who sets an example for others.

December 6, the date of Saint Nicholas's death, became a holiday in many parts of Europe. Children left their shoes out by their fireplaces on the evening of December 5. They believed that Saint Nicholas would ride across the sky on his horse, carrying gifts for good children. In the morning many children found candy and toys in the shoes they had left by their fireplaces.

During the mid-1500s, a new kind of Christianity spread throughout Europe. It was called Protestantism. It was led by a man named Martin Luther, who did not like the

Giving and receiving gifts was not always such an important part of Christmas.

worship of saints. He disliked Saint Nicholas Day because it was in honor of a saint. He also thought the customs of Saint Nicholas Day were childish. Many of his followers thought that children should still receive gifts, though. But they thought the gifts should come directly from a figure that was more closely related to Christmas.

In some countries new gift givers took the place of Saint Nicholas. They were more closely related to Christmas. In Germany the Christ child known as *Christskindl*, brought gifts to children. *Christskindl* means "Christ child" in German. In England children received gifts from Father Christmas. He was a large man dressed in a red robe lined with fur. French children called him *Père Noel*, which

Santa Claus has become an important symbol of Christmas.

Martin Luther was the leader of a new and different kind of Christianity. It spread through Europe in the mid-1500s.

means "Father Christmas" in French. Saint Nicholas was still the gift giver in the Netherlands. Dutch children called him *Sinter Klass*. This is where we get the name Santa Claus.

In 1624, Dutch people settled in what is now New York. They called their colony New Netherland, and they called its capital New Amsterdam. They brought their Saint Nicholas customs with them. Some forty years later, the British took over and renamed the colony New York. They also brought their Christmas customs, including Father Christmas, with them. Father Christmas brought gifts to British children. Saint Nicholas brought gifts to Dutch children. Eventually, the Dutch and British people began to marry each other, and they shared customs. Gradually, Sinter Klass and Father Christmas were blended together into one gift giver. This is the figure we know as Santa Claus.

Father Christmas uses a wooden cane to knock on doors as he delivers gifts.

The man we know as Santa Claus is actually a combination of different gift givers from many different countries.

A young girl holding a doll and a heart sits on Santa's lap. Perhaps she is telling him what she would like for Christmas.

CHAPTER 4

Christmas Grows in America

In the early 1800s many people in the United States still had not started to celebrate Christmas. It was not yet a legal holiday. Children attended school that day and their parents went to work. Some people believed that Christmas celebrations were sinful. Not everyone in the United States knew about Santa Claus. By the end of the 1800s, both Christmas and Santa Claus became popular all over the United States.

An author named Clement Clarke Moore and an artist named Thomas Nast helped to shape the idea of Santa Claus. They helped to make

Christmas more like the holiday that we know today.

While riding home in a sleigh in December 1822, Clement Moore got the idea for a poem about Christmas. He called his poem *A Visit from Saint Nicholas*. You may know this poem as *The Night Before Christmas*. He read the poem to his family and friends on Christmas Eve in 1822. One of his friends liked the poem. She sent a copy of it to a newspaper in Troy, New York.

Close to Christmas Eve in 1823, the newspaper published the poem. Over the next few years, the poem was printed in many newspapers. Millions of people were able to read it. It helped them to see Santa Claus as the figure we know today.

In the early 1800s, not everyone in the United states knew about Santa Claus.

It also gave people the idea of Christmas as a holiday for children to receive gifts.

Between 1863 and 1886, Thomas Nast drew pictures of Moore's creation each year for *Harper's Weekly* magazine. This helped to make Santa Claus famous all across the United States. Sending Christmas cards and decorating Christmas trees also helped Christmas to become more popular. The custom of decorating evergreen trees began in Germany around the 1600s. Soon the custom spread throughout Europe. In 1850 an American magazine printed a picture of Queen Victoria, the queen of England, at Christmas. Her family stood around a Christmas tree. The tree had been decorated by her husband, Prince Albert, who was born in Germany. Some families in the United States copied this idea. During the

Thomas Nast was an artist who helped to shape the idea of Santa Claus.

Today, many people think of Christmas as a time for children to receive gifts from Santa Claus.

1800s, many German people came to live in the United States and they kept this tradition.

The idea of sending Christmas cards began in the early 1800s in England. English schoolboys sent out greetings on decorated paper called Christmas pieces, to their parents. These showed how well the boys could write.

The boys hoped their good handwriting would earn them many Christmas gifts. Adults sometimes sent Christmas verses or messages to friends, too.

In the 1840s the English postal service improved, and it became easier for people to

The idea of sending out Christmas cards began in the early 1800s in England.

Christmas Blessings

Many blessings Christmas brings
On its wide and glowing wings, —
May the brightest of them all
On your path this season fall.

H M Burnside.

MAY CHRISTMAS BE
HAPPY IN SCORES
OF WAYS
AND LAST THROUGH
THREE HUNDRED
AND SIXTY FIVE DAYS

Sending Christmas cards and decorating trees helped to make Christmas popular.

mail cards and letters. One of the officials at the post office had a friend named John Horsely who published children's books and was also an artist. In 1843, Horsely designed and printed about one thousand cards with Christmas themes. The cards were expensive, but they sold well. Soon, many companies began printing Christmas cards.

The first Christmas cards to be sold in the United States came from England. In 1875 a man named Louis Prang began printing Christmas cards in Boston, Massachusetts. Soon he was selling 1 million cards every year. Other companies copied his cards. Today, Christmas cards are used to send holiday wishes to millions of people.

By 1890 the idea of Christmas as a festive holiday was accepted by most people in the United States. It was also a legal holiday in all states and territories by 1890.

Singing Christmas songs, or carols, also became very popular.

Many people decorate outdoor trees like this one at Christmas.

Christmas Now

Most Christmas trees come from tree farms. They take five to fifteen years to grow. More than 30 million trees are sold in the United States each year.

Many people go to church services on Christmas Eve, Christmas Day, and throughout the Christmas season. Many Christians mark the season of Advent, the four weeks of waiting for the birth of Jesus before Christmas. They create an Advent wreath, a wreath of evergreens with four candles standing in the greens. They light one candle on each of the four Sundays before Christmas as they wait for the date of Jesus's birth.

Many people also celebrate the nonreligious aspects of Christmas. They enjoy the holiday

Many people light Advent candles to mark the weeks leading up to the birth of Jesus. One candle is lit on each of the four Sundays before Christmas.

without going to church. They like the feelings of family, kindness, and caring that Christmas is all about. Many modern songs, stories, and movies about Christmas focus on these things.

In 1949 the song "Rudolph the Red-Nosed Reindeer" was recorded. The song is about a reindeer who is teased because he has a big red nose. It is a very popular Christmas song that helps us to think about being kind to all people, including those who are different. "I'll Be Home for Christmas," another song, expresses the idea of wanting to be with one's family during Christmas.

People often say that too many people think of Christmas as a time to spend money on gifts instead of thinking about the reason that Christmas was started. It is true that Christmas decorations may appear

"Rudolph the Red-Nosed Reindeer" is a popular Christmas song. It helps us to think about being kind to all people.

in stores as early as September, three months before the holiday. And people in the United States do spend a lot of money each year on Christmas gifts.

However, the true spirit of Christmas does still exist. Families get together. People give their time and money to help those in need. Many children and adults sing Christmas carols at hospitals and nursing homes.

Many people like to decorate their house with lots of colorful lights.

Some people enjoy the Christmas spirit by going to see the big tree at Rockefeller Center, in New York City.

Sometimes they bring baked goods and gifts. At Christmas many people try to be kinder and more giving to one another. They think about what their friends and families have meant to them throughout the year. These acts of kindness and generosity are what Jesus wanted to teach. It is fitting that people do these things at the time that they celebrate his birth.

At Christmas, many people think about family and friends.

Christmas Craft Project

★

Reindeer Ornament

Reindeer remind us of Christmas. After all, they pull Santa's sleigh. Here is how to make a reindeer ornament to hang on your tree, decorate your home, or give as a gift. You will need:

- ✔ **clean sticks from ice-cream bars or craft sticks**
- ✔ **white glue**
- ✔ **plastic wiggle eyes**
- ✔ **a small red pom-pom**
- ✔ **glitter**
- ✔ **a 6-inch piece of yarn or string**

*Safety Note: Be sure to ask for help from an adult, if needed, to complete this project.

1. Glue the ice-cream or craft sticks together in the shape of a triangle. This forms the head of the reindeer.

2. With the point of the triangle facing down, glue eyes onto the middle of the left and right sticks.

3. Glue the pom-pom onto the bottom point of the triangle to make the nose.

4. Cover sticks with glue. Sprinkle on glitter. Let the glue dry.

5. Tie yarn or string around the top stick, leaving enough string to hang the ornament.

Timeline

★

0—Christ is born in Bethlehem.

A.D. 33—Christ is crucified.

A.D. 336—One of the first Christmas celebrations is held on December 25.

A.D. 343—St. Nicholas dies. The date of his death becomes a holiday in many parts of Europe.

About A.D. 500—Three masses are held for Christmas on December 25.

Mid-1500s—Protestantism forms and spreads throughout Europe. Protestant church leaders feel a figure more closely related to Christmas should replace Saint Nicholas as the one to bring gifts.

Timeline

★

Early 1600s—Dutch settlers come to America. They bring their custom of Saint Nicholas with them. British settlers come to America and bring their custom of Father Christmas. Both figures mix to form what we know as Santa Claus.

Early 1800s—Commercial Christmas cards are invented in England.

1875—The first Christmas cards are printed in the United States.

1890—Christmas becomes a legal holiday in the United States.

Words to Know

★

A.D.—*Anno Domini*, which means "in the year of our Lord." These two letters placed before a year indicate that the date comes after the birth of Christ.

apostles—The closest followers of Jesus Christ.

B.C.—"Before Christ." These two letters placed after a date indicate that the date comes before the birth of Christ.

bishop—A high ranking official in the Catholic Church. He is selected by the pope to be the leader of a local church community.

Christianity—The religion that Jesus Christ founded.

Words to Know

Christmas Eve—The night before Christmas.

manger—A feed box for animals.

nativity scene—A Christmas decoration that shows the birth of Christ in the manger.

pagans—People who believed in more than one god.

saint—A holy person or a religious hero who sets an example for others.

shepherd—Someone who takes care of sheep.

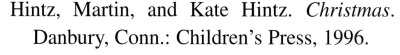

Reading About

Chambers, Catherine. *Christmas*. Orlando, Fla.: Raintree Steck-Vaughn Publishers, 1997.

Hintz, Martin, and Kate Hintz. *Christmas*. Danbury, Conn.: Children's Press, 1996.

Rau, Dana Meachen. *Christmas*. Danbury, Conn.: Children's Press, 2000.

Roop, Peter, and Connie Roop. *Let's Celebrate Christmas*. Brookfield, Conn.: Millbrook Press, 1997.

Ross, Kathy. *Christmas Ornaments Kids Can Make*. Brookfield, Conn.: Millbrook Press, 1998.

Internet Addresses

★

CHRISTMAS TIME AT KID'S DOMAIN
<http://www.kidsdomain.com/holiday/xmas/>

KID'S DOMAIN CHRISTMAS GAMES
<http://www.kidsdomain.com/games/xmas.html>

SANTA'S CHRISTMAS PAGE
<http://www.santaschristmas.ca/>

SANTA'S OFFICIAL WEBSITE
<http://www.northpole4kids.com>

Index